Perfect PENGUINS

ROCKHOPPER PENGUIN

Written by Bethany Latham

Enslow PUBLISHING

Published in 2026 by Enslow Publishing, LLC
2544 Clinton Street
Buffalo, NY 14224

Written by: Bethany Latham
Edited by: Rebecca Phillips-Bartlett
Designed by: Amy Li

Cataloging-in-Publication Data

Names: Latham, Bethany, author.
Title: Rockhopper penguin / Bethany Latham.
Description: Buffalo, NY : Enslow Publishing, 2026. | Series: Perfect penguins | Includes glossary and index.
Identifiers: ISBN 9781978547438 (pbk.) | ISBN 9781978547445 (library bound) | ISBN 9781978547452 (ebook)
Subjects: LCSH: Eudyptes chrysocome--Juvenile literature. | Crested penguins--Juvenile literature.
Classification: LCC QL696.S473 L834 2026 | DDC 598.47--dc23

Manufactured in the United States of America

CPSIA compliance information: Batch #QW26ENS: For further information contact Enslow Publishing LLC, New York, New York at 1-800-398-2504.

IMAGE CREDITS

All images are courtesy of Shutterstock.com, unless otherwise stated.

Recurring – Martyshova Maria (doodles and arrows). Cover – Lee Walker, Giedriius. 2–3 – Danita Delimont. 4–5 – Vladimir Protasov2323, Sadie Whitelocks, Maridav, Daniel Brent, Rob Jansen. 6–7 – Traveller MG, Danita Delimont. 8–9 – Rob Jansen, Birgit Droste. 10–11 – Ondrej Prosicky, Rob Jansen. 12–13 – SJM51, buenaventura. 14–15 – Danita Delimont, Jeremy Richards. 16–17 – Albert 1988, Giedriius. 18–19 – semper-scifi, Right Cameraman, Riaan van den Berg. 20–21 – Danita Delimont, Christian Vinces. 22–23 – Ondrej Prosicky, Jeremy Richards.

CONTENTS

WORDS THAT LOOK LIKE THIS CAN BE FOUND IN THE GLOSSARY ON PAGE 24.

ROCKHOPPER PENGUINS

Penguins are a type of flightless bird. Instead of flying through the air, they use their flippers to move through the water. There are 18 different species of penguins.

EMPEROR PENGUIN

GALAPAGOS PENGUIN

ADÉLIE PENGUIN

NORTHERN ROCKHOPPER

SOUTHERN ROCKHOPPER

Rockhopper penguins are some of the smallest penguins in the world. They grow to around 20 inches (50 cm) tall. There are different types of rockhopper. These include the northern rockhopper and southern rockhopper.

HABITAT

Rockhopper penguins live on and around rocky islands and coasts. They spend lots of time on slopes with patches of long grass. However, northern and southern rockhoppers live in different parts of the world.

An animal's natural home is called its habitat.

Northern rockhoppers prefer living in cool habitats. They live on islands in the South Atlantic Ocean and Indian Ocean. Southern rockhoppers live in warmer places. They live around lower South America.

BODY

Northern and southern rockhoppers look very similar. They have red eyes, pink feet, and reddish-orange beaks. Rockhoppers can change the shape of their eyes' lenses to help them see clearly in and out of water.

Rockhopper penguins are best known for the long yellow feathers that grow on their heads. They look like eyebrows. They also have spiky black feathers on the back of their heads. These make a crest.

GETTING AROUND

Rockhoppers are good swimmers and divers. Their dives are often quite shallow. However, rockhoppers can dive down to around 330 feet (100 m) underwater to find food. Rockhopper penguins swim faster than they walk.

Rockhopper penguins are very lively. They travel around the rocky slopes by jumping from rock to rock with their feet together. This is why they are called rockhopper penguins.

LIFE CYCLE

A life cycle is the stages of an animal's life that lead to the animal having their own young.

Rockhopper penguins usually go back to the same nest each year to mate. They often mate with the same penguin every year.

Rockhopper penguins' nests are dips in the ground filled with leaves and rocks. The mother usually lays two eggs. The second egg is always bigger. The mother and father take turns looking after the eggs.

To find a mate, rockhopper penguins shake their eyebrows.

After about 32 days, the eggs hatch. For three weeks, the father looks after the chicks while the mother finds food. Rockhopper penguin chicks are gray, white, and fluffy. They don't have their eyebrows yet.

Once they leave the nest, rockhopper penguin chicks gather in groups called crèches to keep safe. Their parents return to the sea to hunt. Rockhopper penguins can have young when they are four years old.

FAMILY LIFE

Rockhopper penguins are very protective of their eggs and chicks. Parents peck predators with their beaks to keep them away. They sometimes fight with other rockhopper penguins for food and nesting spots.

Rockhopper penguins fight by slapping each other with their flippers.

Rockhopper penguins are very loud. They call, or bray, to each other. Sometimes, they do this to tell each other where they are. Other times, they do it to tell another penguin to go away.

DIET AND DANGERS

Northern and southern rockhopper penguins' diets include lots of krill. They also eat young squid and small fish. Rockhopper penguins spend three to five months at sea every year hunting for food.

A diet is the type of food an animal eats.

In the ocean, rockhopper penguins face danger from southern sea lions and leopard seals. On land, eggs and chicks are in danger of being eaten by birds, such as skuas and gulls.

PROTECT THE PENGUINS

Northern rockhopper penguins are endangered. This means they are at risk of dying out. Southern rockhopper penguins are vulnerable. This means their numbers are falling but they are not likely to die out soon.

Climate change and people fishing too much affect how much food rockhopper penguins can find. Rockhoppers also face danger from oil spills. Some people are working on making safe areas in the ocean to protect the penguins.

PERFECT PENGUINS

Rockhopper penguins are perfectly lively birds. We have seen how they hop around to climb rocky slopes and explore. How do you keep active?

Rockhopper penguins' habitats need a lot of looking after. How could you help stop pollution to protect the penguins?

What was your favorite rockhopper penguin fact? Do you think you would like to meet a rockhopper penguin?

GLOSSARY

CLIMATE CHANGE	a change in the typical weather or temperature of a large area
COASTS	where the land meets the sea
CREST	a section of feathers, fur, or skin on the top of an animal's head
LENSES	parts of the eye that direct light onto the back of the eye
MATE	to produce young with an animal of the same species
OIL SPILLS	when oil leaks into the sea or other types of water, such as a lake
POLLUTION	harmful and poisonous things being added to an environment
PREDATORS	animals that hunt other animals for food
SHALLOW	not very deep
SPECIES	a group of very similar animals or plants that can create young together

INDEX